TO ROBERT

    ON YOUR

FROM St LEONARDS CULLOM,

    SCHOOL.

  22nd OCTOBER, 2000.

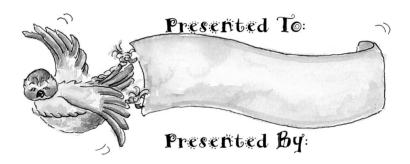

Presented To:

Presented By:

_____

Date:

_____

God's Little Story Book about Jesus

Tulsa, Oklahoma

Stories based on the following Bible versions:

The Holy Bible, New International Version®. NIV®. Copyright © 1973, 1978, 1984 by International Bible Society. Used by permission of Zondervan Publishing House. All rights reserved.

The *King James Version* of the Bible.

God's Little Story Book about Jesus
ISBN 1-56292-611-X
Copyright © 2000 by Honor Books
P.O. Box 55388
Tulsa, OK 74155

Written by Sarah M. Hupp
Cover and Interior Design by Whisner Design Group
Illustrated by Lisa Browning

introduction

This is the story of Jesus. He is God's special gift to every person in the world.

Our story begins with the amazing birth of Jesus. It tells about the wonderful ways Jesus helped people. It also tells how much Jesus loved His Heavenly Father, God. He wanted everyone to know that God really loved them.

Jesus is still alive and lives in a beautiful place called Heaven. He loves you very much. You will love Him, too, as you read His story.

Contents

jesus is Born

(Luke 2:1-7)

Mary and Joseph went to Bethlehem to pay taxes. Mary rode on a donkey. She was going to have a baby. The baby was God's Son.

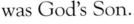

9

Bethlehem was full of people. Mary and Joseph could not find a place to sleep. Mary said, "Joseph! The baby wants to be born. We must find a place to stay!"

A kind man told them they could sleep with his animals. So Mary had her baby in a stable and laid Him in the hay. She named the baby Jesus.

Dear God, thank You for the kind man who shared his stable. Help me to be kind and share, too.
Amen.

12

The Bright Star and the Sheep

(Luke 2:8-20)

One cold night, shepherds were taking care of their sheep. They looked up and saw a bright star in the sky. Then the whole sky filled up with singing angels. The men were afraid!

13

An angel said, "Don't be afraid. I have good news. A baby is born in Bethlehem. He is Jesus, the Lord. You will find Him in a manger asleep in the hay."

Then the angels went back up into Heaven.

And the men went to look for Jesus.

Thank You, God, for the stars at night.
When I look at them, I will think about Jesus.
Amen.

The Wise Men

(Matthew 2:1-12)

Some wise men, who lived far away, saw the same star. They climbed on their donkeys. They climbed on their camels. And they followed that bright star to Israel.

The star guided them to Bethlehem. It stopped right over the place where baby Jesus was born. The wise men said, "Where is the new King? We saw His star in the sky. We came to worship Him."

When the wise men saw Jesus with Mary, they bowed. They gave Jesus lots of presents. Everyone was happy that Jesus was born!

Dear Lord, I can give You a present, too. I can give You my heart! I love You, Jesus.
Amen.

Jesus in the Temple

(Luke 2:41-52)

When Jesus was twelve years old, He went to the Temple with Mary and Joseph. They went to pray and give God an offering. When Mary and Joseph started back home, they thought Jesus was with their group. He wasn't! Mary was so worried. Where could He be?

21

Mary and Joseph looked and looked for Jesus. Finally, they went back to the Temple. They found Jesus talking to the teachers about God. He was very wise for His age. Everyone was so surprised!

Mary scolded Jesus for making her worry. But He told her that He had been doing His Father's business. Remember? He was God's Son.

Dear God, You kept Jesus safe when He was lost.
Thank You for keeping me safe, too.
Amen.

John Baptizes Jesus

(John 1:29-34)

A man named John camped by the river. He told people to follow God. He told them to stop doing wrong things and start obeying God. Then he baptized them in water.

》

Jesus went to see John. He wanted to be baptized, too, even though He had never done anything wrong. John said, "You are the Lamb of God. You will take away the sins of the world."

When Jesus came out of the water, a dove flew down from Heaven. It landed on Jesus. And God said, "This is My Son. I love Him. He makes Me happy."

Dear God, help me to be like Jesus.
I want to make You happy, too.
Amen.

Twelve Helpers

(Matthew 4:18-21; John 1:35-51)

One day, Jesus was walking by the Sea of Galilee. Andrew saw Him and spoke to Him. Then Andrew went to find his brother, Peter. Andrew brought Peter to Jesus. And they both became Jesus' disciples (helpers and students).

Jesus also saw James and John, who were fishing. He said to them, "Come! Follow Me!" Right away, they got out of their boat and followed Him. They became disciples, too.

Jesus asked twelve men to follow Him. They all became His disciples. He taught them about God every day. And they told other people about God, too.

Dear God, I'm glad Jesus had disciples. Teach me how I can help others, too.
Amen.

31

Four Friends

(Luke 5:17-26)

A man wanted to go see Jesus. But he could not walk. His legs were hurt. So his friends picked him up and carried him on his bed. They took him to see Jesus.

Jesus was talking to a house full of people. The friends tried and tried, but they could not get inside. Then the four friends had an idea.

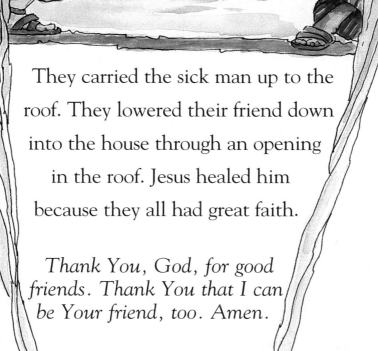

They carried the sick man up to the roof. They lowered their friend down into the house through an opening in the roof. Jesus healed him because they all had great faith.

Thank You, God, for good friends. Thank You that I can be Your friend, too. Amen.

35

You Must Be Born Again

(John 3:1-21)

Nicodemus was a wise teacher and a good leader. And he knew Jesus had great power from God. One night, he came to visit Jesus. Nicodemus wanted to know more about God.

Jesus said, "You must be born again."
Nicodemus did not know what Jesus
was talking about. "I have already
been born," he said. Jesus
smiled. "You must be born
again in your heart."

Then Jesus said to Nicodemus, "God loves you. He sent His Son to save you. If you believe in Me, you will live forever." Nicodemus believed Jesus.

Dear Lord, thank You for loving me.
I'm sorry that I do wrong things.
I want to be born again.
Come and live in my heart.
Amen.

The Lady at the Well

(John 4:4-42)

One day, a woman was getting some water from a well. Jesus said, "If you drink this water, you will be thirsty again. But if you drink the water that I have, you will never be thirsty."

41

The woman did not know what Jesus was talking about. So Jesus said, "The water I have is living water. You can have it, too. Trust in Me."

Jesus told her all about how she was living wrongly. It surprised her that Jesus knew all about her life. So she said, "I want this water." And she went and told her friends about Jesus.

Dear Lord, I want living water, too. Then my heart will never be thirsty again. Help me to trust in You always. Amen.

43

A Scary Storm

(Mark 4:35-41)

Jesus and His disciples got into a boat to cross the Sea of Galilee. Jesus was very tired, so He went to sleep in the back of the boat. His friends rowed and rowed.

Then a big storm came up. The wind blew hard. The waves got bigger and bigger! But Jesus kept on sleeping. The disciples were afraid!

They woke up Jesus. They said, "Don't You care if the boat sinks?" Jesus looked around. Then He said, "Wind! Waves! Stop!" And the storm stopped!

Wow! Jesus, I'm glad You're stronger than storms. You took care of Your friends. You can take care of me, too. Amen.

48

i Can See

(John 9:1-34)

Jesus met a man who could not see. He could not see the sky. He could not see the trees. He could not see Jesus. The man was blind. Jesus put some mud on the man's eyes. Then Jesus said, "Go! Wash the mud off."

The man did what Jesus told him. And when he opened his eyes, he could see everything! Jesus had healed his eyes!

The man was so happy! He ran to tell

everyone, saying, "I was blind. But now I can see.

Praise God!"

Thank You, Lord, for my eyes.
Thank You that I can see, too.
Amen.

God Takes Care of You

(Matthew 6:25-30)

Jesus told people not to worry. But some people worried a lot. They worried about food. They worried about clothes. They did not know what would happen to them. And this made them feel afraid.

53

Jesus said to them, "Don't worry. God takes care of the flowers. And He takes care of the birds. He knows what you need, too. God will take care of you."

54

Then Jesus said, "Keep your eyes on God. Keep on doing what is right. And everything you need will be given to you, too."

Dear Lord, I'm glad I don't need to worry about anything. Thank You for giving me everything I need. Amen.

A Lost Sheep

(Luke 15:1-7)

Jesus told this story:

A man took good care of his sheep. One night, he saw that one of his sheep was missing. Where could it be? He went to look for the lost sheep. He looked and looked.

When he found the lost sheep, he carried it home. He said to his friends, "Look! Be happy! I found my lost sheep!"

When we tell God we are sorry for the things we have done wrong, He is so happy! He is as happy as the man who found his lost sheep. And the angels in heaven are happy, too!

Dear Lord, I'm sorry for the
bad things I do.
Help me to be more like You
every day.
Amen.

A Lost Coin

(Luke 15:8-10)

Jesus told this story:

A woman had ten pennies. It was all the money she had. But something happened. She lost one of the pennies! She swept her house. She looked under the bed. She looked and looked until she found the lost coin.

When the woman found the penny, she was happy. She told her friends, "I lost my penny. But now I have found it. Be happy with me!"

Jesus said, "God and the angels are happy, too, when someone turns away from doing bad things."

*Dear God, I want You to be happy.
Help me to be good. Amen.*

One Man Says Thanks

(Luke 17:11-19)

Ten men were very sick. When they saw Jesus walking by, they yelled, "Jesus! Help us!" Jesus saw the men and felt sorry for them. He said, "Go to the priest in the Temple." The men did what Jesus said. And as they were on their way, they were healed.

One man saw that he was no longer sick. He ran back to Jesus. He hugged Jesus' feet and said, "Thank You! Thank You!"

He was the only one of the ten men who said thank You. Jesus said, "Your faith has made you well. Stand up and go home." And the man did.

Thank You, Lord, for all You do.
Thank You for loving me.
Thank You for my family, too. Amen.

A Friend Dies

(John 11:1-44)

Lazarus was a good friend of Jesus. But Lazarus got sick and died while Jesus was on a trip. Lazarus' sisters put his body in a cave.

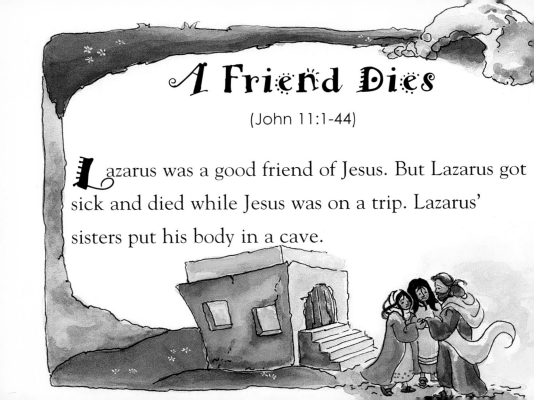

After a few days, Jesus finally got to their house. His sisters said, "If you had been here, Lazarus would not have died."

But Jesus said, "He will live again. If anyone trusts in Me, they will live even if they die."

Jesus went to the cave. He prayed, "God, thank You for hearing me. Let these people trust in me." Then Jesus said, "Lazarus! Come out!" And Lazarus came out of the cave. He was alive again!

Dear Lord, thank You for hearing my prayers, too. I trust in You. Amen.

Jesus and the Children

(Mark 10:13-16)

People brought their children to Jesus so He could bless them. Jesus loved children. And children loved Jesus. They liked to talk to Him and sit on His lap. Jesus made them feel special.

But Jesus' disciples told the children to go away. They said Jesus was too busy. This made Jesus angry.

He said, "Let the children come! People must learn to love God like children do."

Then Jesus hugged the children. He put His hands on them and blessed them.

Thank You, Jesus, for loving me.
Thank You for hearing my prayers. I love You!
Amen.

A Little Man

(Luke 19:1-10)

Jesus was coming to town! People were so excited. They gathered on the roadside so that they could watch for Him. But Zacchaeus could not see Jesus. The people were too tall. And Zacchaeus was too short.

Zaccheus ran down the road, jumping up to see. Then he got an idea. He climbed up a tree and looked down. Now he could see Jesus!

When Jesus walked by, He looked up and saw Zacchaeus. He smiled and said, "Zacchaeus! Come down! I want to stay at your house." So Zacchaeus climbed down from the tree. And they went to his house together.

*Dear Lord, I'm glad You love
short people.
I'm glad You love me, too.
Amen.*

A Donkey Ride

(Luke 19:28-44)

Many people loved Jesus and knew He was the promised Savior. So when Jesus wanted to go into the city, a kind man gave Him a donkey. People laid palm branches down on the road to honor Jesus. The road was very dusty. And they did not want Jesus to get dirty.

As Jesus rode the donkey into the city, people began to praise God. They told each other about all the wonderful things Jesus had done.

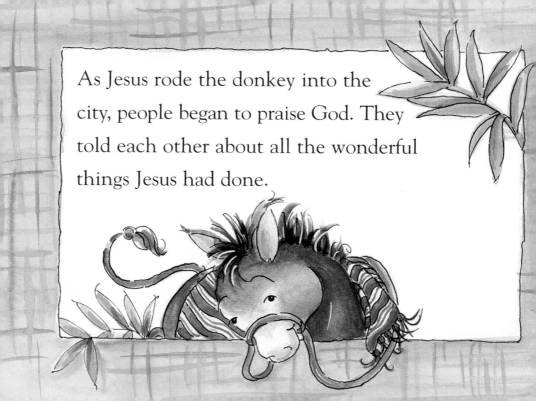

The people shouted, "Hosanna! Give God glory!
Give blessing to the One who comes in the name of
the Lord!"

*Praise You, Lord! Hosanna! I give You glory!
You are great! I love You. Amen.*

A Supper with Friends

(Matthew 26:17-30)

Jesus and His friends gathered around the supper table. Jesus knew He was going to die soon. So He wanted to spend time with His best friends.

Jesus picked up some bread and thanked God for it. Then Jesus broke the bread in half. He said, "Eat this. It is My body. It is broken for you."

Then Jesus picked up His cup. He thanked God for it, too. Jesus said, "Drink from this cup. This cup is My blood. My blood will be poured out so that many people can be forgiven for their sins."

Dear Lord, thank You for dying for me.
Thank You for forgiving
my sins. Amen.

Jesus Prays

(Matthew 26:36-56)

*A*fter supper, Jesus and His friends went to a garden. Jesus said, "I want to pray. Stay awake and pray with Me." So Jesus went to a quiet place and began to pray.

Jesus knew that God wanted Him to die on the cross. He knew that it would be a hard thing to do.

So Jesus prayed, "Father, I don't want to do this. But if this is what You want Me to do, I will do it. I will do what You want Me to do."

Dear Lord, help me to do what You want me to do—even when it seems hard. Amen.

The Cross

(Mark 15:1-39)

The people who hated Jesus took Him to the ruler of the city. The ruler looked at Jesus. He said, "Are You the King of the Jews?" And Jesus said, "Yes. I am."

The ruler said to the people, "This man has done nothing wrong. What do you want me to do with Him?" And the people yelled, "Put Him on a cross! Kill Him!"

So soldiers put a crown of thorns on Jesus' head. They nailed His hands and feet to a cross. They laughed at His pain. Finally, Jesus died.

Dear Lord, those people were so mean.
I'm sorry that I'm mean sometimes, too.
Amen.

Jesus Lives Again

(Matthew 27:57-28:10)

After Jesus died on the cross, a friend put His body in a cave. A large stone was rolled in front of the opening. Then the friends of Jesus cried and went home.

A few days later, some women went to the cave. But the stone was rolled away!
An angel sat on it. The cave was empty. Jesus' body was gone!

The angel said, "I know you are looking for Jesus. He is not here. He is alive again! Go tell His friends!" So the women ran home and told everyone, "Jesus is alive!"

Hurray! Jesus is alive!
Thank You, God, for this good news! Amen.

Jesus and Thomas

(John 20:24-30)

The friends of Jesus
were so happy!
He was alive!

Some of them saw Him in the garden. Some saw Him walking along the road. It was a great day!

But Thomas did not see Jesus. He said, "I will not believe that Jesus is alive unless I see Him. I will not believe what you say unless I can touch Him."

Then Jesus' friends met in a house.
Thomas was with them. While they were
talking, Jesus entered the room. Jesus said,
"Thomas! Touch My hands. Touch My side.
Believe in Me!" And Thomas did.

*Dear Lord, I'm glad that Thomas finally
believed in You. I believe in You, too.
Amen.*

Going Home to Heaven

(Luke 24:45-53; Acts 1:4-11)

Jesus talked to His friends about God and His Word. And Jesus said, "I want you to tell people about Me. I will give you the power to do it."

105

Jesus told His friends to go to Jerusalem. He said, "Wait there until I give you the Holy Spirit. Then Jesus prayed for His friends.

And while Jesus was praying, He went up into Heaven. Then His friends went into the city and praised God.

Dear Lord, help me to learn more
about God every day.
And help me to tell others about You, too.
Amen.

Jesus Will Return

(Revelation 21:3-7; 22:7-21)

Heaven is a beautiful place. There is nothing in Heaven to make you sad or cry. You cannot fall down and skin your knees there. And the sun shines all the time. People who love God will live in Heaven someday.

Jesus lives in Heaven now. He sits next to
God the Father and prays for us.

Jesus says, "I am making everything brand new! And I will come back soon. You will be blessed if you follow My words. Remember! I am coming soon!"

Dear Lord, I miss You. I want You to come back soon.
I want to give You a big hug.
I love You, Jesus! Amen.

If you have enjoyed this book, or if it has
impacted your life, we would like to hear from you.
Please contact us at:

Honor Books
Department E
P.O. Box 55388
Tulsa, Oklahoma 74155

Additional copies of this book and other titles
in the *God's Little Story Book* series
are available from your local bookstore.